Words of Importance

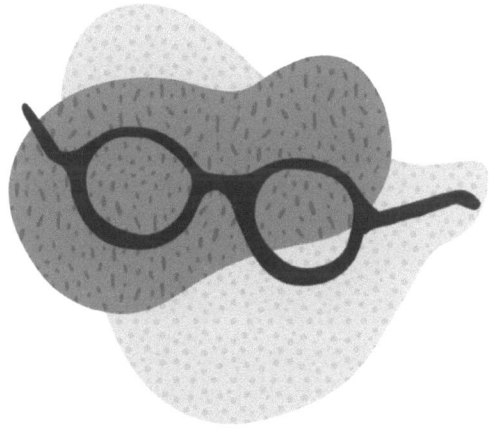

Words of Importance

AJ Publications | Addison Joyner

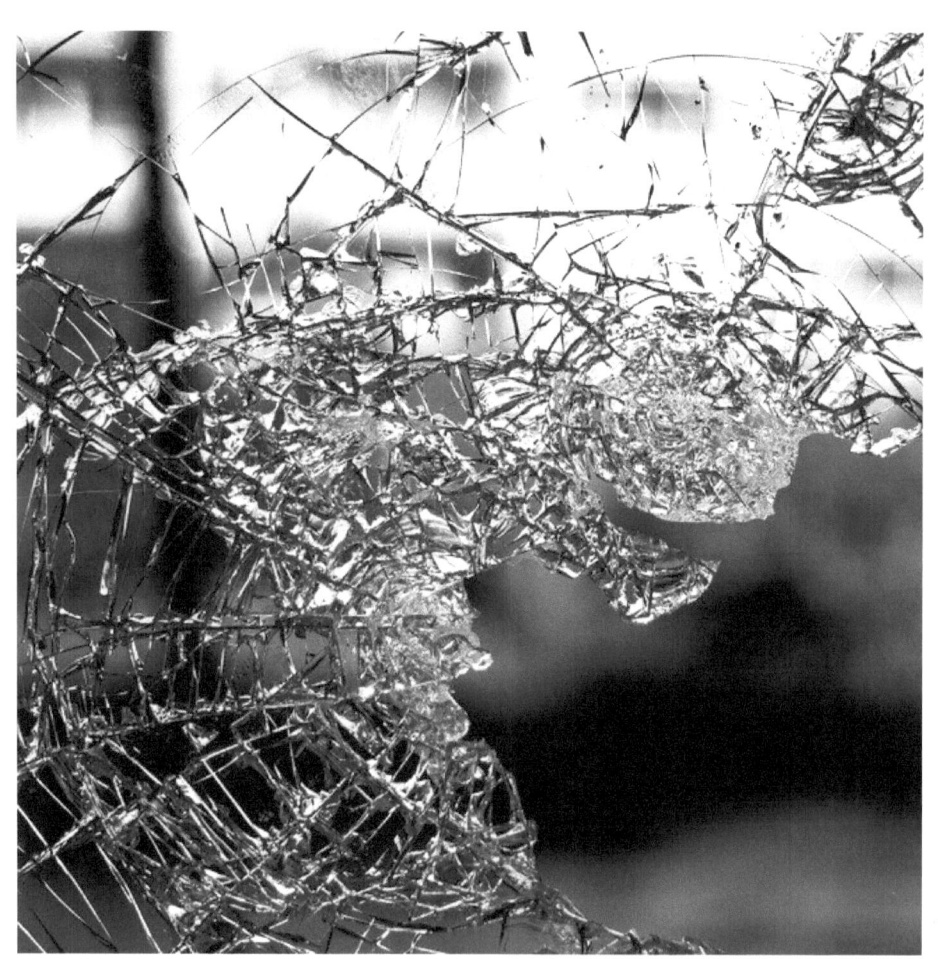

4

Words of Importance
Introduction

Within this book you will find a compiled list of words that are of the utmost importance. Words that have slipped through the cracks of many people's vocabulary. These words have both great significance and great wisdom wrapped within their meanings. The value they hold within the christian life is unquestionable, and to know them is to gain much wisdom and insight.

Each word is defined as Noah Webster originally found sutable in 1828. That being said, the defenitions can be complex, but through studying they can be fully understood. This is a beginning look into the world of lost words.

Their is an additional word towards the end introduced into our language by the great C.S. Lewis. This word explains and unravels much of the complexities loss of language.

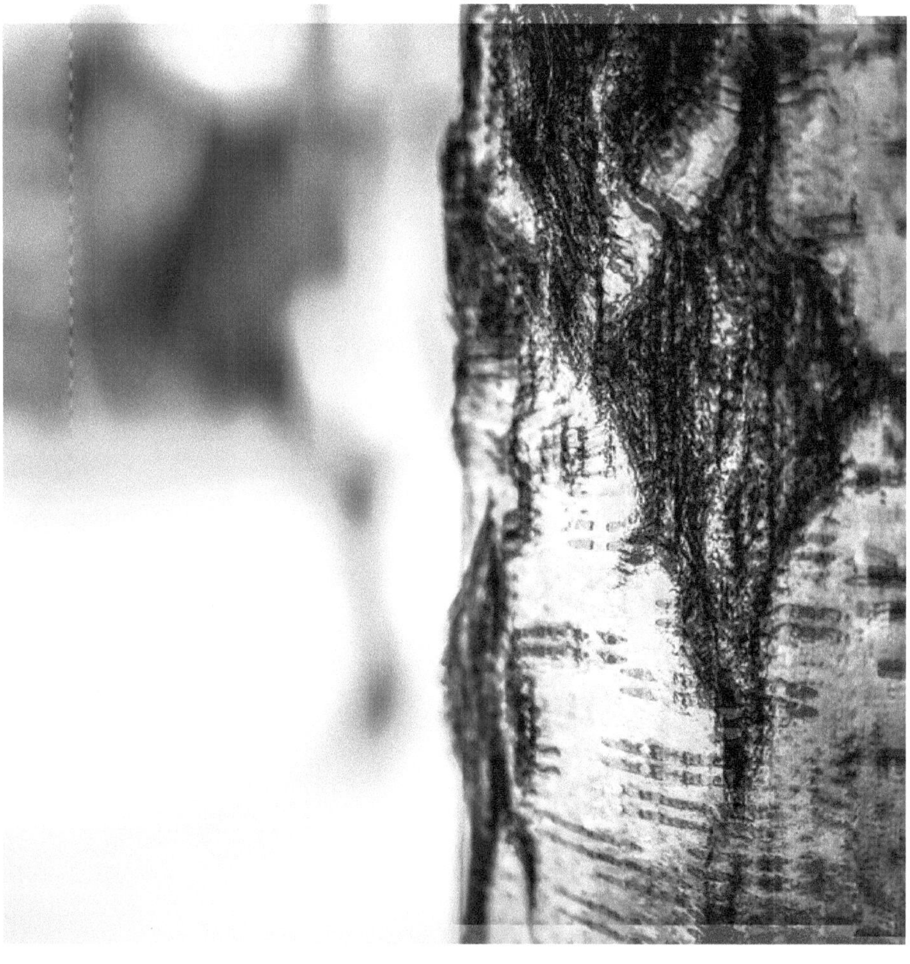

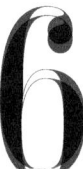

Awful
adjective;

That strikes with awe; that fills with profound reverence; as the awful majesty of Jehovah. Struck with awe; scrupulous. That fills with terror and dread; as the awful approach of death.

7

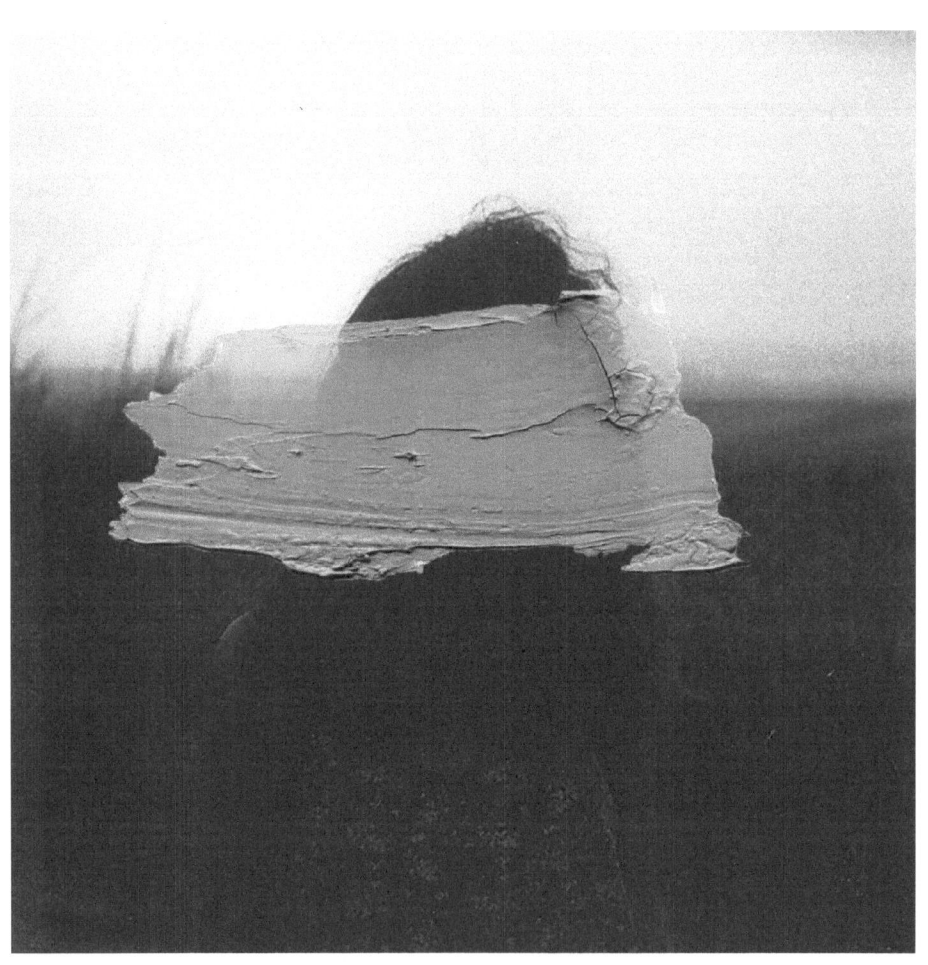

8

Chastity

noun;

Purity of the body; freedom from all unlawful commerce of sexes. Before marriage, purity from all commerce of sexes; after marriage, fidelity to the marriage bed. Freedom from obscenity, as in language or conversation. Freedom from bad mixture; purity in words and phrases. Purity; unadulterated state; as the chastity of the gospel.

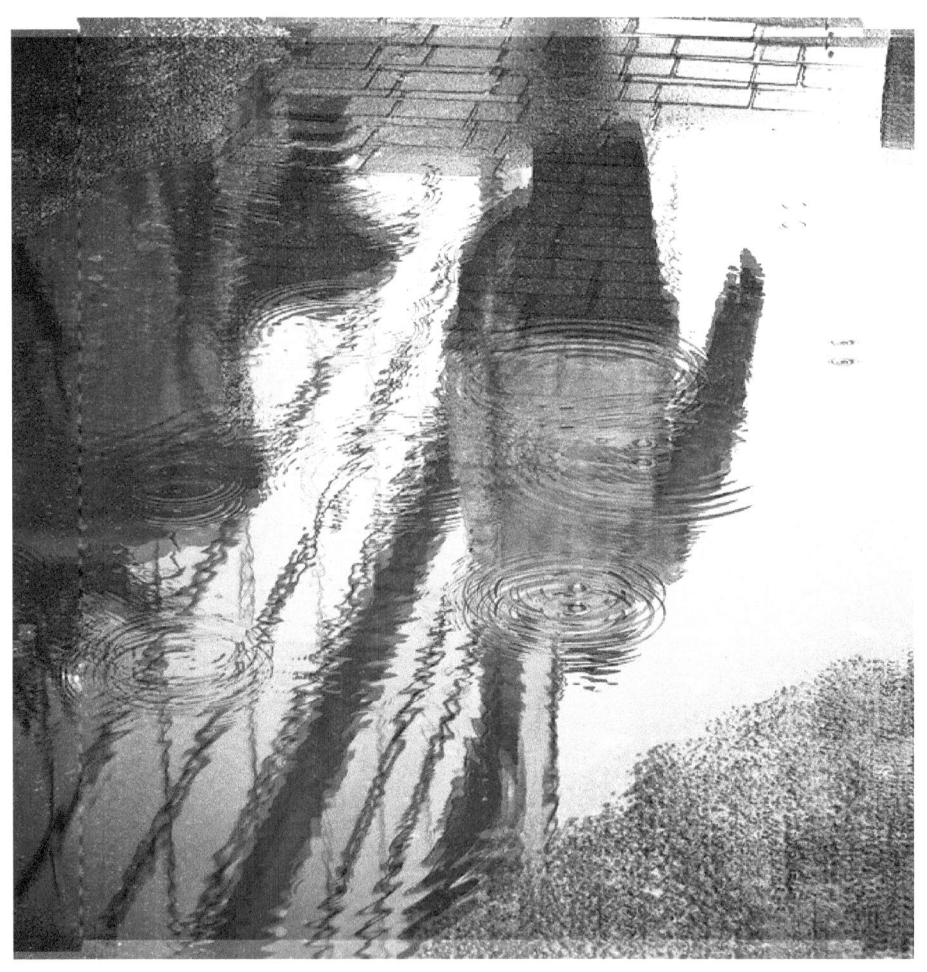

10

Disrepute
noun;

Loss or want of reputation; disesteem; discredit; dishonor. The alchimist and his books have sunk into disrepute

11

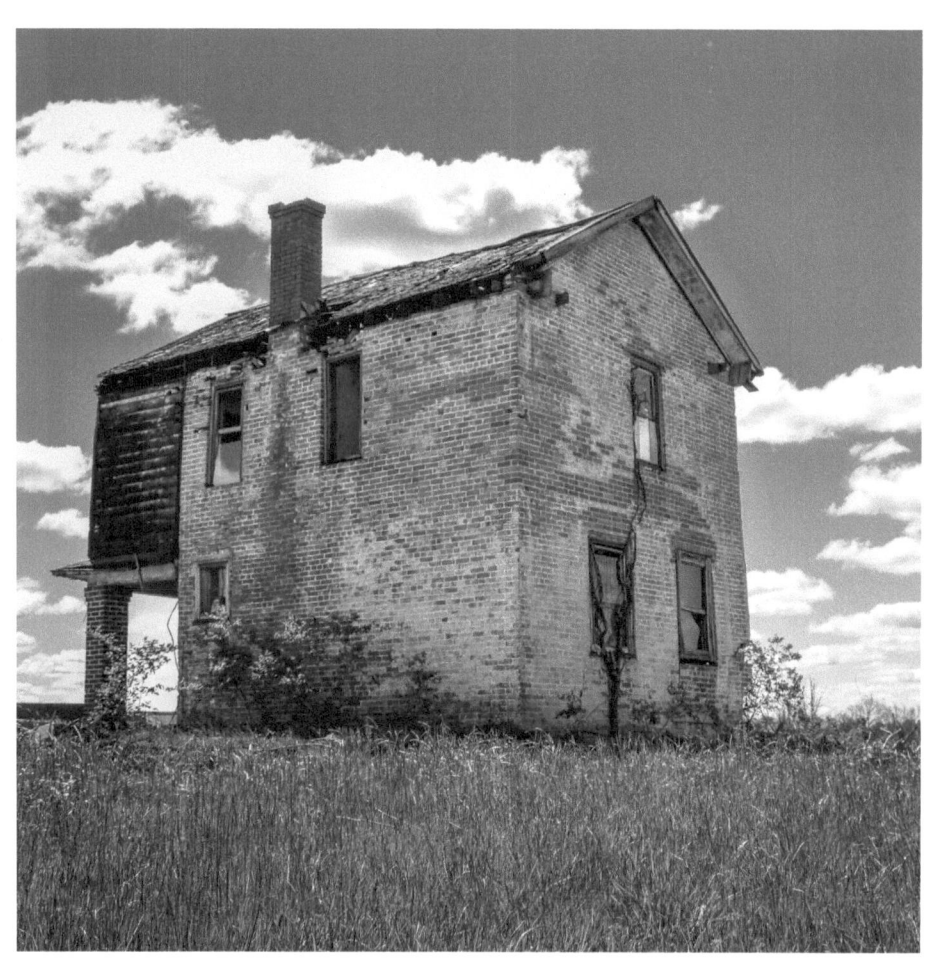

12

Education

noun;

The bringing up, as of a child, instruction; formation of manners. education comprehends all that series of instruction and discipline which is intended to enlighten the understanding, correct the temper, and form the manners and habits of youth, and fit them for usefulness in their future stations.

To give children a good *education* in manners, arts and science, is important; to give them a religious *education* is indispensable; and an immense responsibility rests on parents and guardians who neglect these duties.

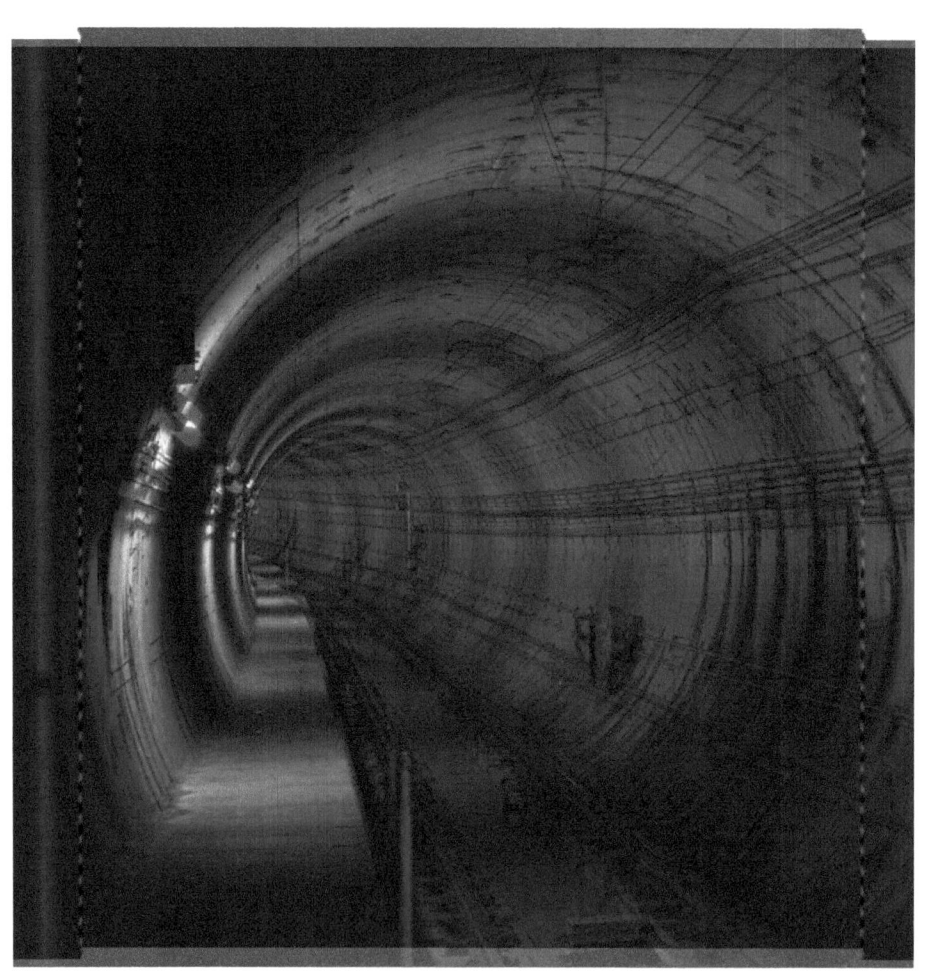

14

Evil
noun;

Natural evil is any thing which produces pain, distress, loss or calamity, or which in any way disturbs the peace, impairs the happiness, or destroys the perfection of natural beings.

Moral evil is any deviation of a moral agent from the rules of conduct prescribed to him by God, or by legitimate human authority; or it is any violation of the plain principles of justice and rectitude.

Having bad qualities of a natural kind; mischievous; having qualities which tend to injury, or to produce mischief. Having bad qualities of a moral kind; wicked; corrupt; perverse; wrong.

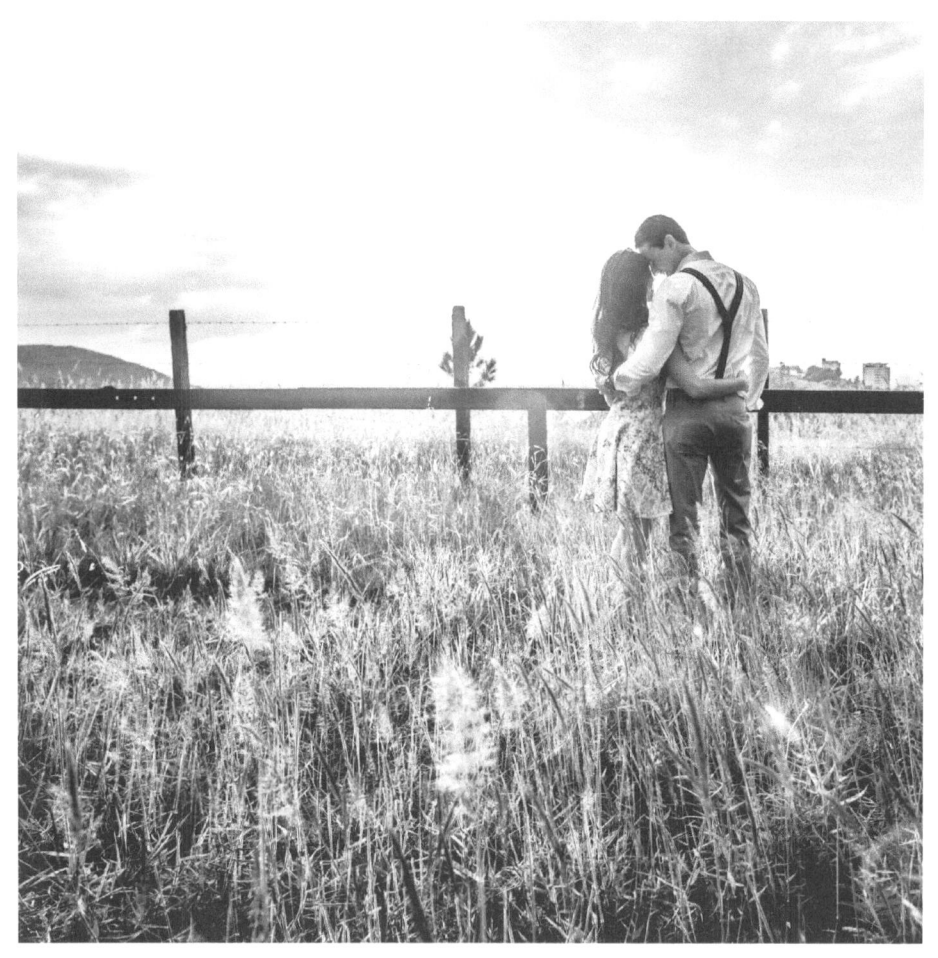

16

Fidelity

noun;

Faithfulness; careful and exact observance of duty, or performance of obligations. We expect fidelity in a public minister, in an agent or trustee, in a domestic servant, in a friend.

　　The best security for the fidelity of men, is to make interest coincide with duty. Observance of the marriage covenant; as the fidelity of a husband or wife.

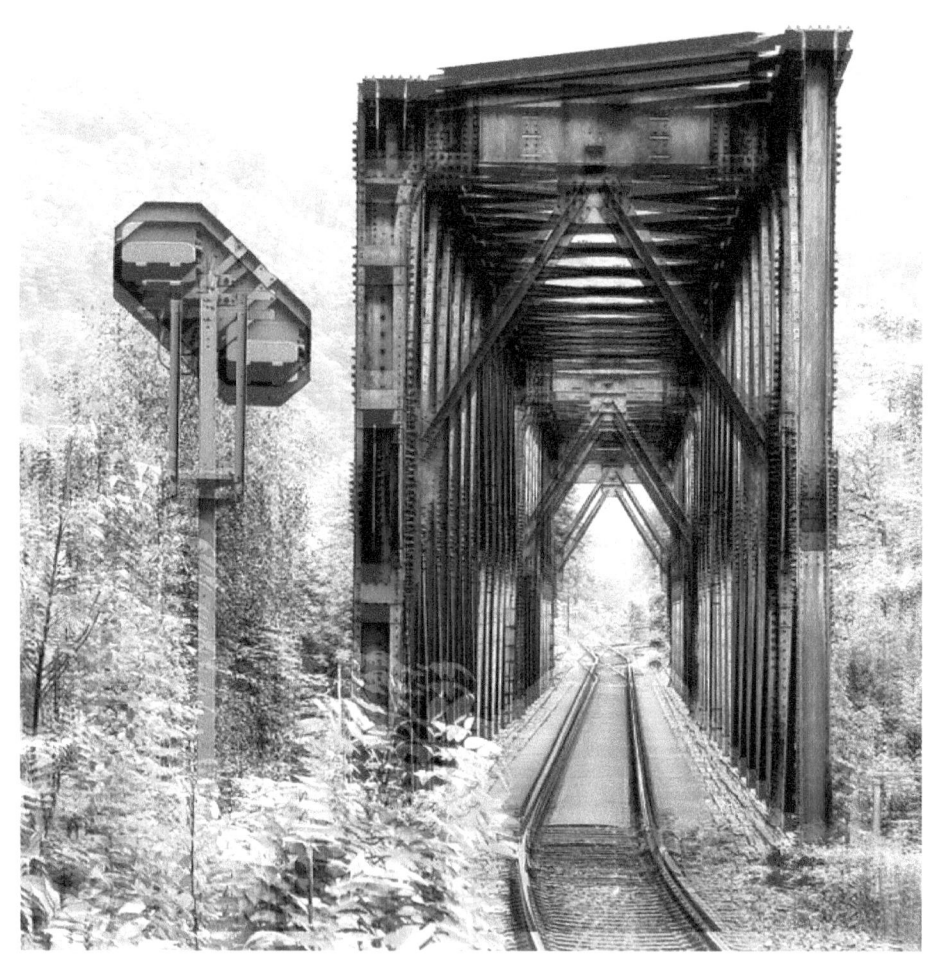

18

Grace
noun;

Favor; good will; kindness; disposition to oblige another; as a grant made as an act of grace. Appropriately, the free unmerited love and favor of God, the spring and source of all the benefits men receive from him. Favorable influence of God; divine influence or the influence of the spirit, in renewing the heart and restraining from sin.

19

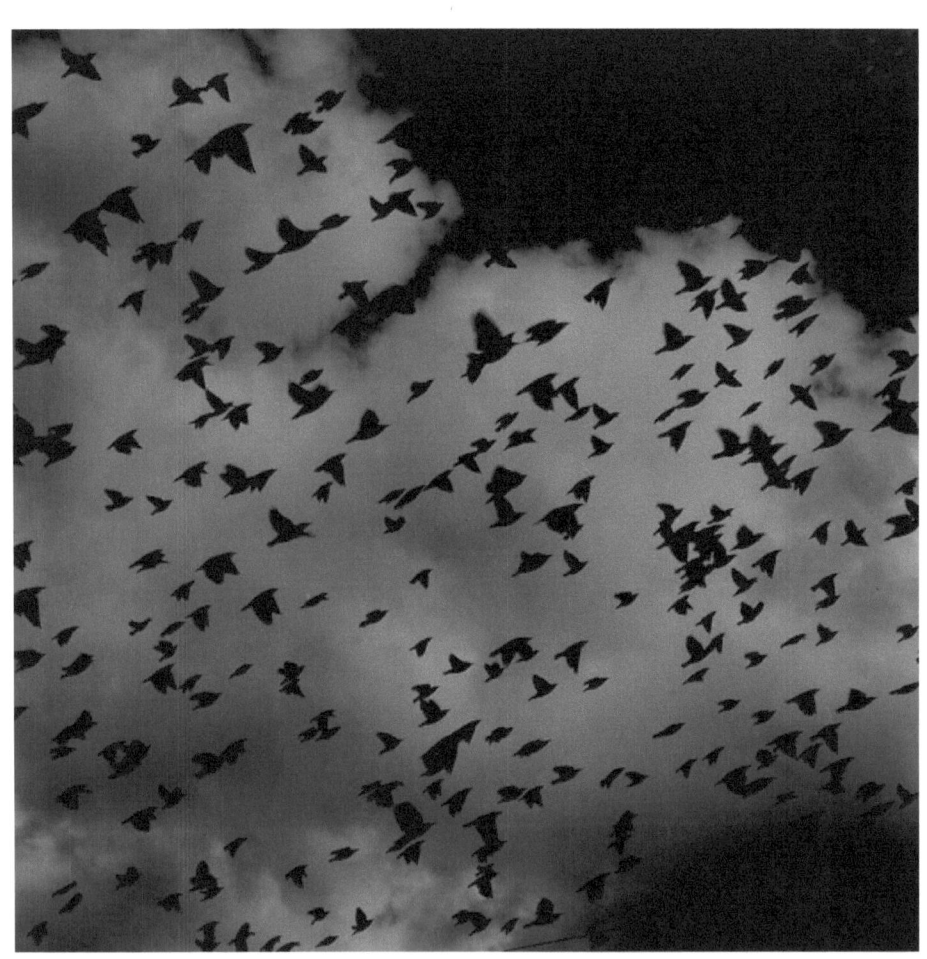

20

Haughty

noun;

Proud and disdainful; having a high opinion of one's self, with some contempt for others; lofty and arrogant; supercilious. Proceeding from excessive pride, or pride mingled with contempt; manifesting pride and disdain; as a haughty air or walk.

22

Justice

noun;

The virtue which consists in giving to every one what is his due; practical conformity to the laws and to principles of rectitude in the dealings of men with each other; honesty; integrity in commerce or mutual intercourse. Justice is distributive or commutative.

Distributive *justice* belongs to magistrates or rulers, and consists in distributing to every man that right or equity which the laws and the principles of equity require; or in deciding controversies according to the laws and to principles of equity. Commutative *justice* consists in fair dealing in trade and mutual intercourse between men.

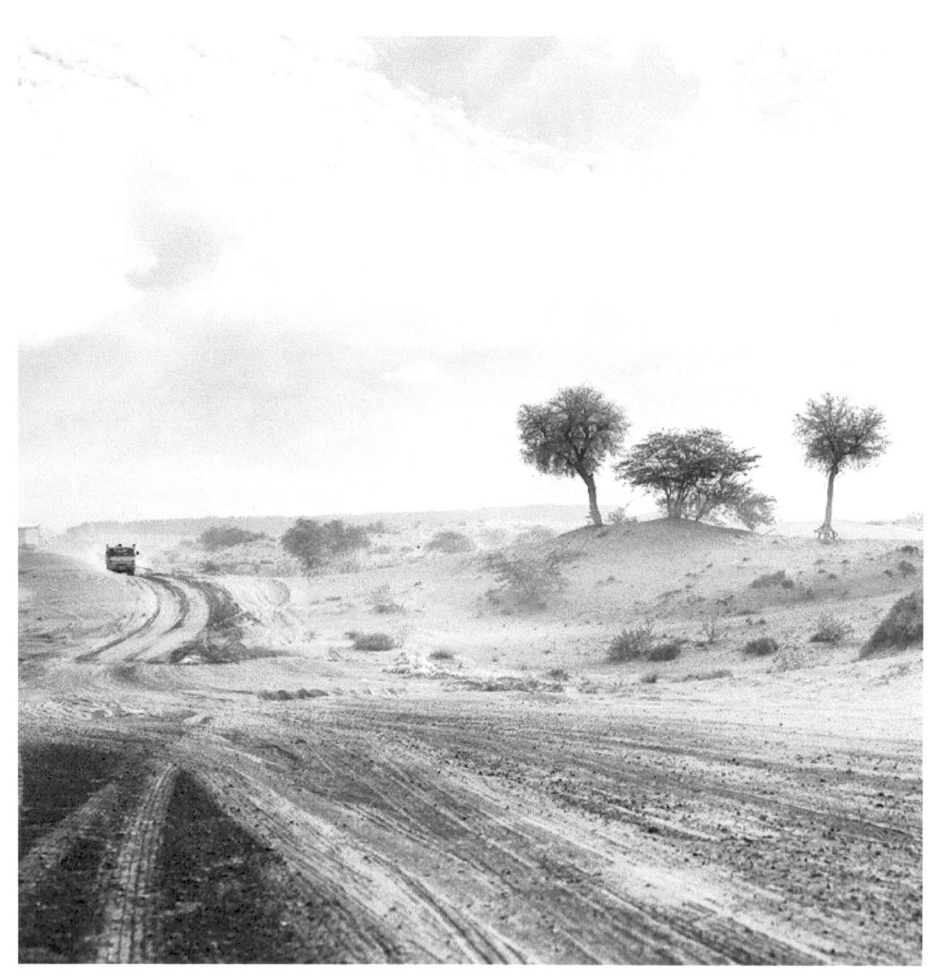

24

Merit

noun;

Goodness or excellence which entitles one to honor or regard; worth; any performance or worth which claims regard or compensation; applied to morals, to excellence in writing, or to valuable services of any kind.

    Thus we speak of the inability of men to obtain salvation by their own merits. We speak of the merits of an author; the merits of a soldier, etc.

26

Mercy

noun;

That benevolence, mildness or tenderness of heart which disposes a person to overlook injuries, or to treat an offender better than he deserves; the disposition that tempers justice, and induces an injured person to forgive trespasses and injuries, and to forbear punishment, or inflict less than law or justice will warrant. In this sense, there is perhaps no word in our language precisely synonymous with mercy. That which comes nearest to it is grace. It implies benevolence, tenderness, mildness, pity or compassion, and clemency, but exercised only towards offenders. mercy is a distinguishing attribute of the Supreme Being.

27

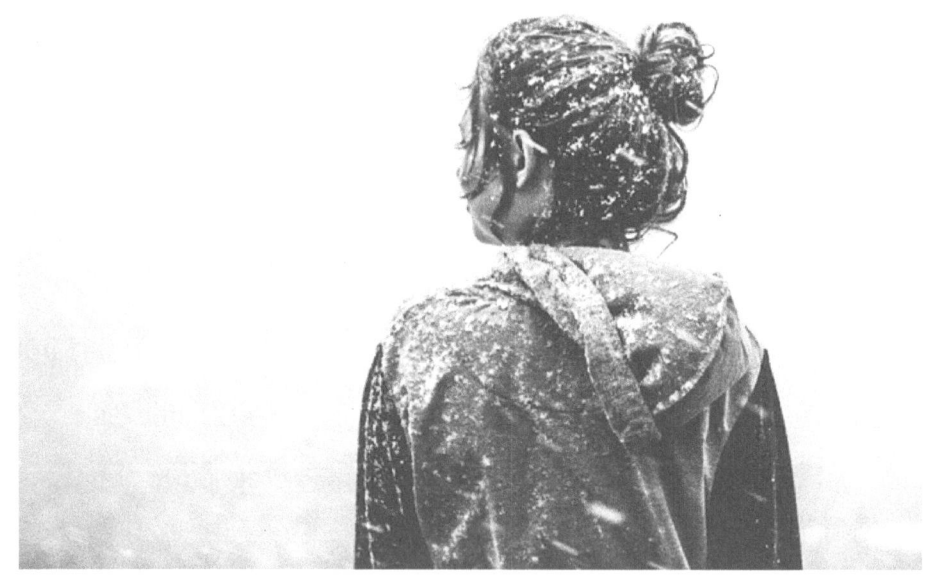

28

Peace

noun;

In a general sense, a state of quiet or tranquillity; freedom from disturbance or agitation; applicable to society, to individuals, or to the temper of the mind. Freedom from agitation or disturbance by the passions, as from fear, terror, anger, anxiety or the like; quietness of mind; tranquillity; calmness; quiet of conscience. Heavenly rest; the happiness of heaven.

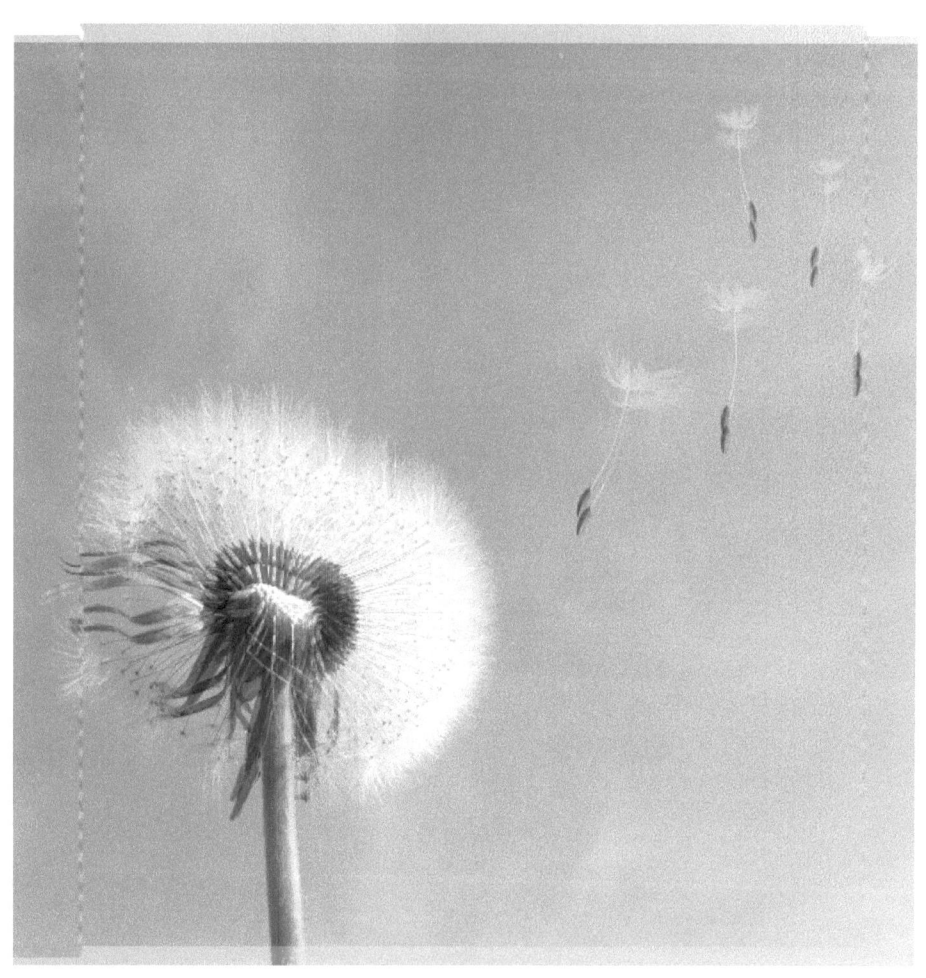

30

Reverence

verb;

To regard with reverence; to regard with fear mingled with respect and affection. We reverence superiors for their age, their authority and their virtues. We ought to reverence parents and upright judges and magistrates. We ought to reverence the Supreme Being, his word and his ordinances.

31

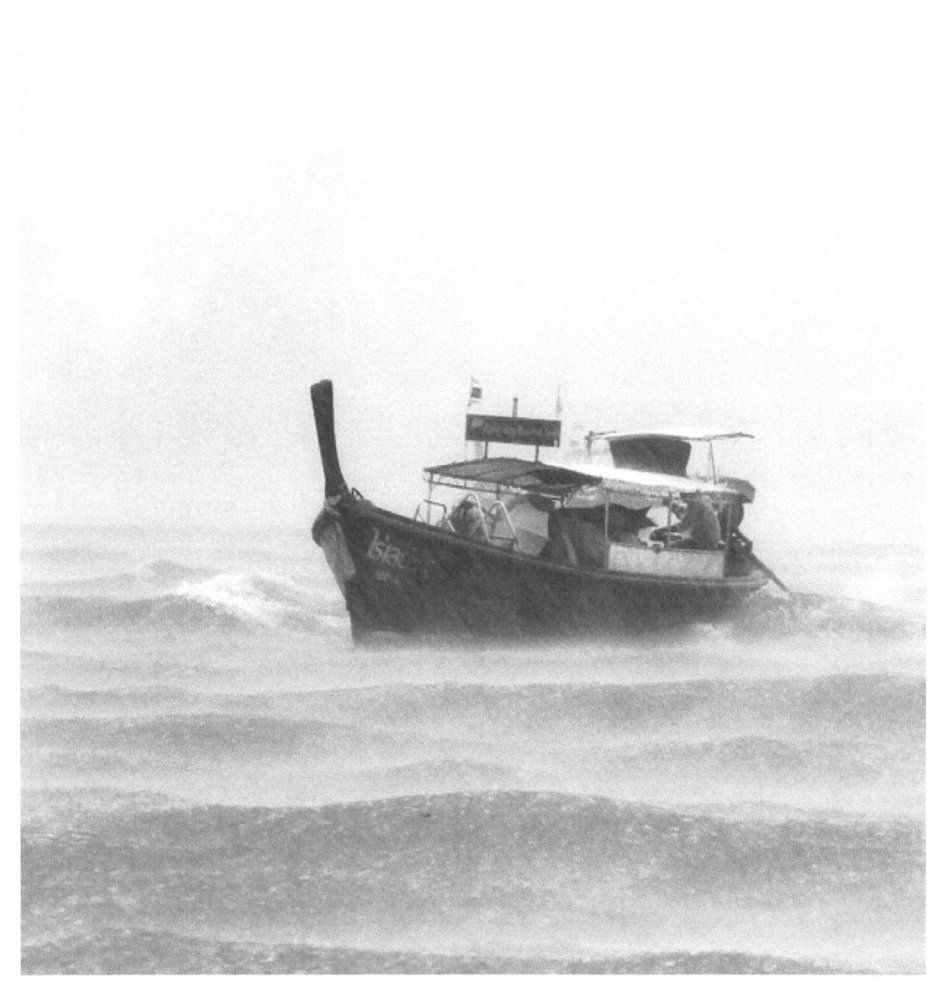

32

Submission

noun;

The act of submitting; the act of yielding to power or authority; surrender of the person and power to the control or government of another. Obedience; compliance with the commands or laws of a superior. submission of children to their parents is an indispensable duty.

Resignation; a yielding of one's will to the will or appointment of a superior without murmuring. Entire and cheerful submission to the will of God is a christian duty of prime excellence.

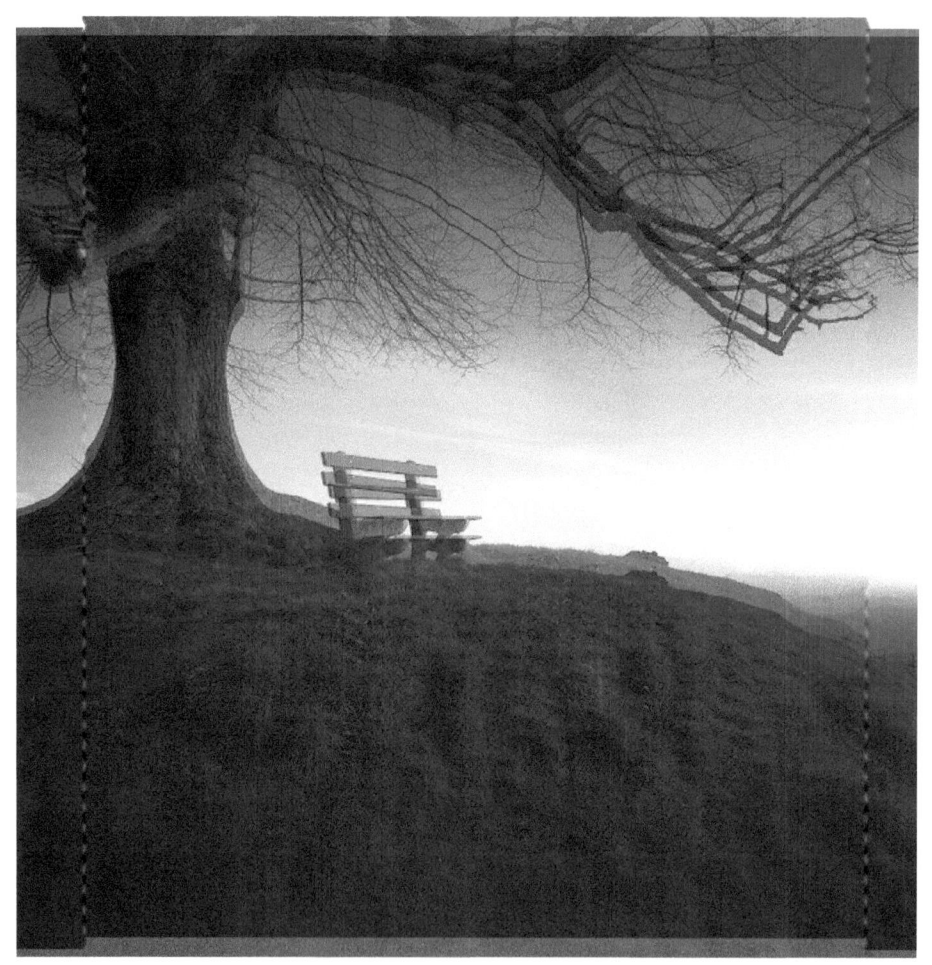

34

Verbicide

verb;

The murder of a word, happens in many ways. Inflation is one of the commonest; those who taught us to say awfully for 'very', tremendous for 'great', sadism for 'cruelty', and unthinkable for 'undesirable' were verbicides.

Another way is verbiage, by which I here mean the use of a word as a promise to pay which is never going to be kept. The use of significant as if it were an absolute, and with no intention of ever telling us what the thing is significant of, is an example.

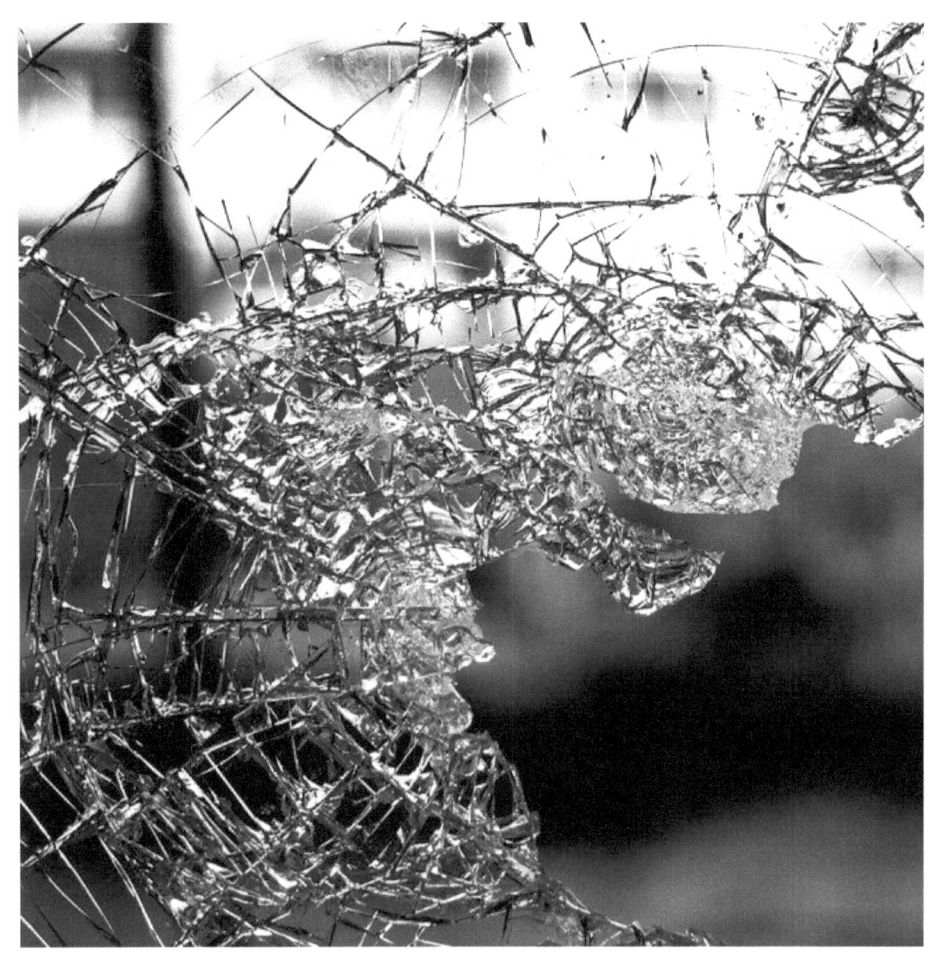

36

Sources

Webster, Noah. An American Dictionary of the English Language. S. Converse, 1828.

C.S. Lewis, Studies in Words. Cambridge University Press, 1960

Images sourced from:
"2.2 Million+ Free Stock Photos for Download - Pixabay." Pixabay, pixabay.com/photos/.

Definitions sourced from:
Webster, Noah. An American Dictionary of the English Language. S. Converse, 1828.
C.S. Lewis, Studies in Words. Cambridge University Press, 1960.

Design by Addison Joyner.

Copyright by Addison Joyner,

First print-on-demand edition published April, 2021.
Every reasonable attemp has been made to identify owners of copyright. Errors or omisions will be corrected in subsequent printings and editions.

AJ Publications

www.ingramcontent.com/pod-product-compliance
Lightning Source LLC
Chambersburg PA
CBHW051934210526
45473CB00006B/2243